King Cobra

The World's Longest Venomous Snake

by Leon Gray

Consultant: Johan Marais
Herpetologist

BEARPORT
PUBLISHING

New York, New York

Credits

Cover, © Indiapicture/Alamy; TOC, © Eric Isselée/Shutterstock; 4–5, © Mandal Ranjit/FLPA; 6, © Patrick Aventurier/Getty Images; 8, © PUMPZA/Shutterstock; 9, © Pat Morris/ardea.com; 10, © Indiapicture/Alamy; 11, © A. Periam Photography/Shutterstock; 12, © iStockphoto/Thinkstock; 13, © Frankiesvacation.com; 14, © Matt Jeppson/Shutterstock; 15, © Olivier Born/Biosphoto/FLPA; 16, © photonewman/Shutterstock; 17, © David Kleyn/Alamy; 18, © Sandesh Kadur/naturepl.com; 19, © P. Gowri Shankar/ www.kalingafoundation.com; 20, © Sandesh Kadur/naturepl.com; 21, © P. Gowri Shankar/www.kalingafoundation.com; 22L, © Robin Winkelman/Dreamstime.com; 22C, © Christopher Murray/Wikimedia; 22R, © Ryan M. Bolton/Shutterstock; 23TL, © Angelo Giampiccolo/ Shutterstock; 23TR, © f9photos/Shutterstock; 23BL, © Matt Jeppson/Shutterstock; 23BR, © Olivier Born/Biosphoto/FLPA.

Publisher: Kenn Goin
Senior Editor: Joyce Tavolacci
Creative Director: Spencer Brinker
Photo Researcher: Calcium Creative

Library of Congress Cataloging-in-Publication Data in process at time of publication (2013)
Library of Congress Control Number: 2012034284
ISBN-13: 978-1-61772-732-0 (library binding)

For more information, write to Bearport Publishing Company, Inc., 45 West 21st Street, Suite 3B, New York, NY 10010. Printed in the United States of America.

10 9 8 7 6 5 4 3 2 1

Contents

Long and Deadly

The king cobra is the longest **venomous** snake in the world.

The deadly cobra is about as long as a pickup truck.

King cobras can grow to be 18 feet (5.5 m) long. They can weigh more than 40 pounds (18 kg).

5

Wet Homes

King cobras live in Southeast Asia.

These huge snakes are found in wet **rain forests**.

King cobras make their homes in trees, bushes, or tall grasses.

King cobras often swim in rivers and streams. They glide across the water by quickly moving their long bodies from side to side.

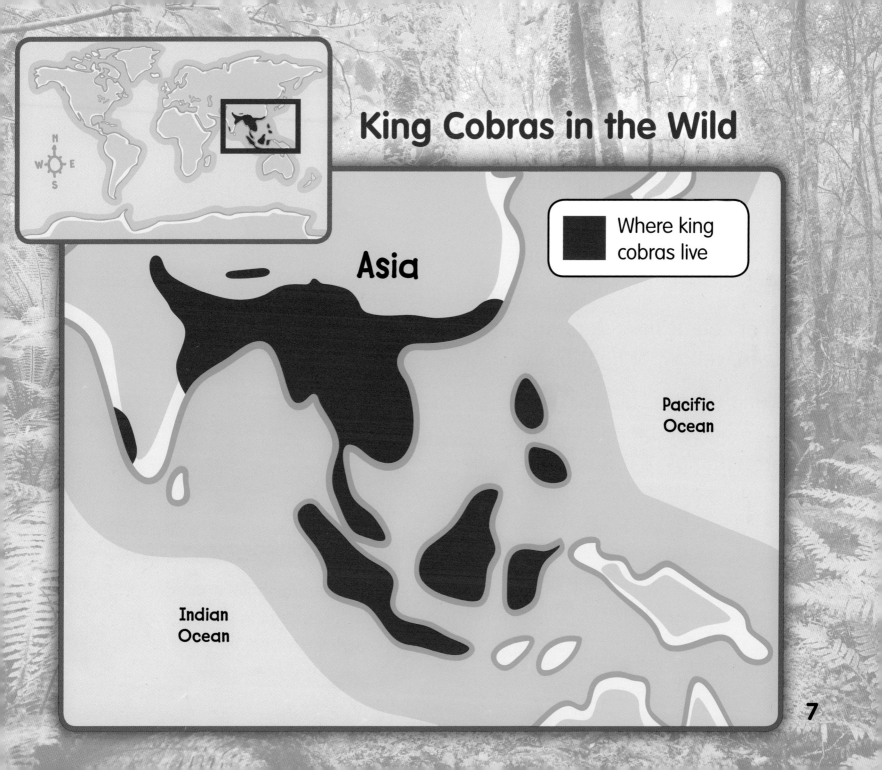

King Cobras in the Wild

Where king cobras live

Asia

Pacific Ocean

Indian Ocean

7

Colorful Cobra

King cobras come in a variety of colors.

Some snakes have skin that is black or dark brown.

Other cobras have skin that is pale green, yellow, or light brown.

A king cobra's colorful skin often helps it blend in with its surroundings as it hunts.

scales

King cobras have hundreds of tiny overlapping plates called scales covering their bodies.

Finding Dinner

King cobras are excellent hunters.

They use their keen eyesight to locate an animal as far away as 330 feet (100.6 m).

That is a distance longer than a football field!

Cobras also use their tongues to smell **prey** that is nearby.

They flick their forked tongues in and out of their mouths.

This helps them to pick up animal smells in the air.

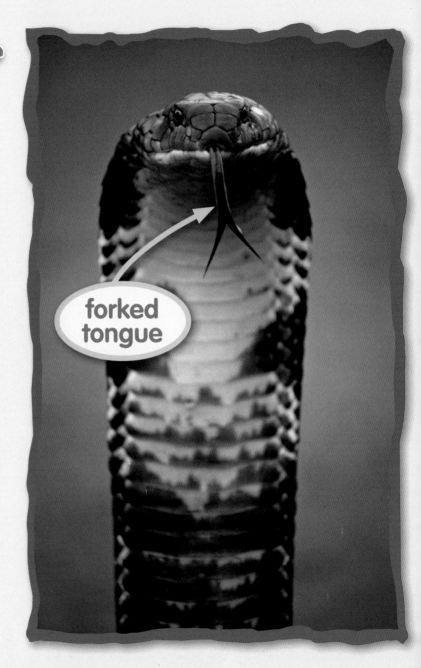

forked tongue

Like all snakes, king cobras do not have ears on the outside of their bodies. However, using bones inside their jaws, they can feel the movements of animals nearby.

Going In for the Kill

Once it finds food, a king cobra bites its prey.

The huge snake has two short, sharp **fangs** in its mouth.

As the cobra bites, its fangs squirt a deadly poison called venom into its victim.

The venom causes the animal to stop moving.

Then, the king cobra eats its prey whole.

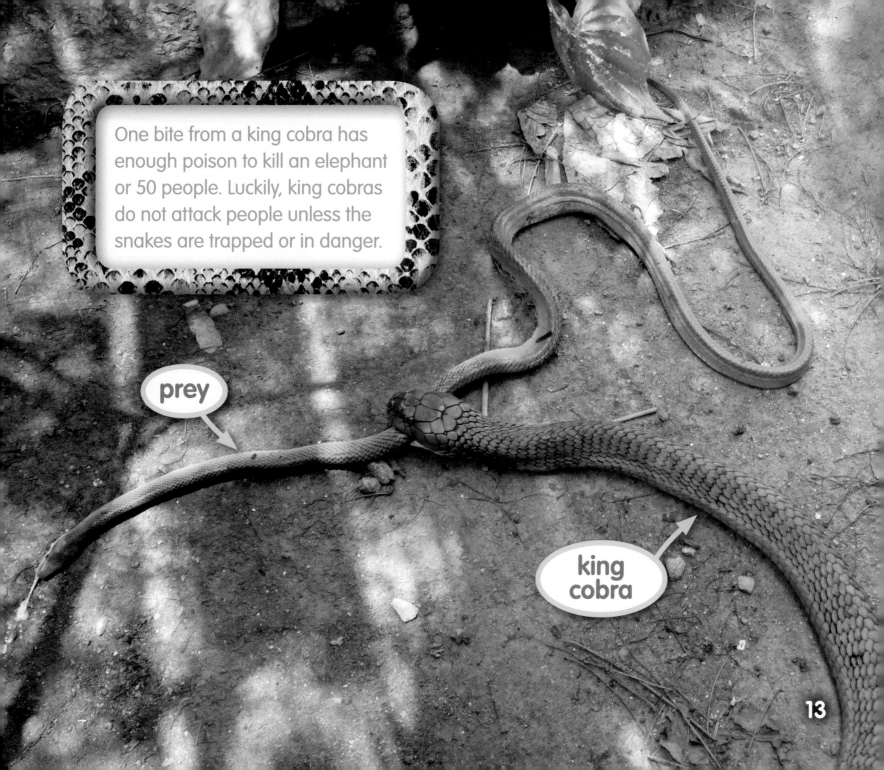

One bite from a king cobra has enough poison to kill an elephant or 50 people. Luckily, king cobras do not attack people unless the snakes are trapped or in danger.

prey

king cobra

13

A Giant Meal

Other snakes are the king cobra's favorite food.

It eats rat snakes, pythons, and even other cobras.

It can take up to an hour for a king cobra to swallow a large snake.

Afterward, the king of snakes might not eat again for another month.

Snakes have teeth, but they cannot chew. Instead, a snake moves its jaws from side to side to push an animal down its throat.

rat snake

jaws

On Guard!

A king cobra not only kills prey, it will also fight enemies, such as crocodiles.

Before fighting, however, the cobra tries to scare enemies away.

First, it raises its head and growls like a dog.

Next, to make itself look bigger, the cobra flattens the skin around its neck called a hood.

Finally, if the enemy is not scared away, the snake attacks with its fierce fangs.

crocodile

The giant snake can lift the front one-third of its body up to six feet (1.8 m) off the ground! That is about as tall as a grown person.

17

A Snake's Nest

Mother cobras guard their babies—even before they are born.

A female king cobra lays between 20 and 50 eggs at a time.

She covers them with leaves and then lies on the eggs to keep them safe.

If an attacker tries to eat the eggs, the mother cobra growls and raises her hood.

eggs

mother cobra

nest

A king cobra is the only kind of snake that makes a nest and guards its eggs. Many other types of snakes leave their eggs after laying them.

Little Killers

About two months after the eggs are laid, baby king cobras push out of their shells headfirst.

Each baby is more than one foot (30.5 cm) long.

The baby king cobra can already make venom.

In a few days, it will be ready to hunt for prey.

It can take up to ten years for a cobra to become fully grown and the king of all snakes.

baby cobra hatching

A baby king cobra can stick out its tongue, spread its hood, and growl just like an adult.

hood

baby cobras

More Long Venomous Snakes

A king cobra is a kind of snake. All snakes belong to a group of animals called reptiles. Most reptiles hatch from eggs. Reptiles have dry, flat skin covered with scales. They are also cold-blooded animals, which means their bodies are as warm or as cold as the places where they live.

Here are three more long venomous snakes.

Black Mamba

The black mamba is the world's second-longest venomous snake. It can grow to be 14 feet (4.3 m) long.

Bushmaster

The bushmaster is found in Central and South America and can grow up to 12 feet (3.6 m) long.

Eastern Diamondback Rattlesnake

The eastern diamondback rattlesnake can grow to be 8 feet (2.4 m) long.

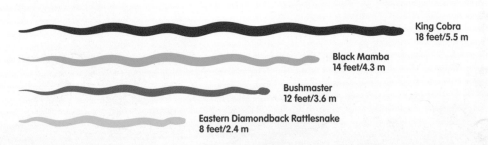

King Cobra
18 feet/5.5 m

Black Mamba
14 feet/4.3 m

Bushmaster
12 feet/3.6 m

Eastern Diamondback Rattlesnake
8 feet/2.4 m

Glossary

fangs (FANGZ) sharp, pointed teeth that some snakes use to pump poison into animals

rain forests (RAYN FOR-ists) warm places where many trees grow and a lot of rain falls

prey (PRAY) animals that are hunted and eaten by other animals

venomous (VEN-uh-muhss) full of poison

Index

Read More

Graham, Audry. *King Cobra (Killer Snakes).* New York: Gareth Stevens (2011).

Gunderson, Megan M. *King Cobras (Checkerboard Animal Library: Snakes).* Edina, MN: ABDO (2011).

Owings, Lisa. *The King Cobra (Pilot Books: Nature's Deadliest).* Minneapolis, MN: Bellwether Media (2012).

Learn More Online

To learn more about king cobras, visit
www.bearportpublishing.com/EvenMoreSuperSized